LITTLE BIG BOOK PLUS

Table of Contents

Animal Tracks 3
nonfiction by Arthur Dorros

Fast Facts: Cottontails 32
an article by Claire Miller
from Ranger Rick *magazine*

Whatsit? 36
an identification puzzle
from Owl *magazine*

Hiding 38
a guessing game
from Your Big Backyard *magazine*

Meet Arthur Dorros

Arthur Dorros had different kinds of pets growing up, including thirteen box turtles. Since he couldn't tell the turtles apart, he named each of them Bobby!

When Mr. Dorros was five, he would look for animal tracks near his house. This book is based on those adventures.

Animal Tracks

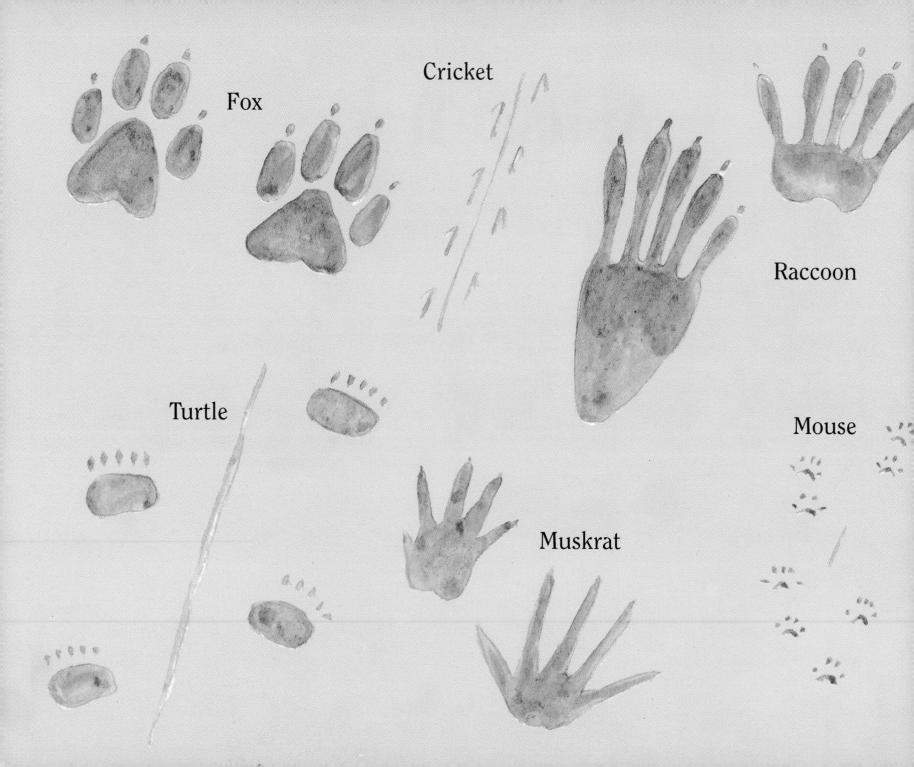

Fox

Cricket

Raccoon

Turtle

Mouse

Muskrat

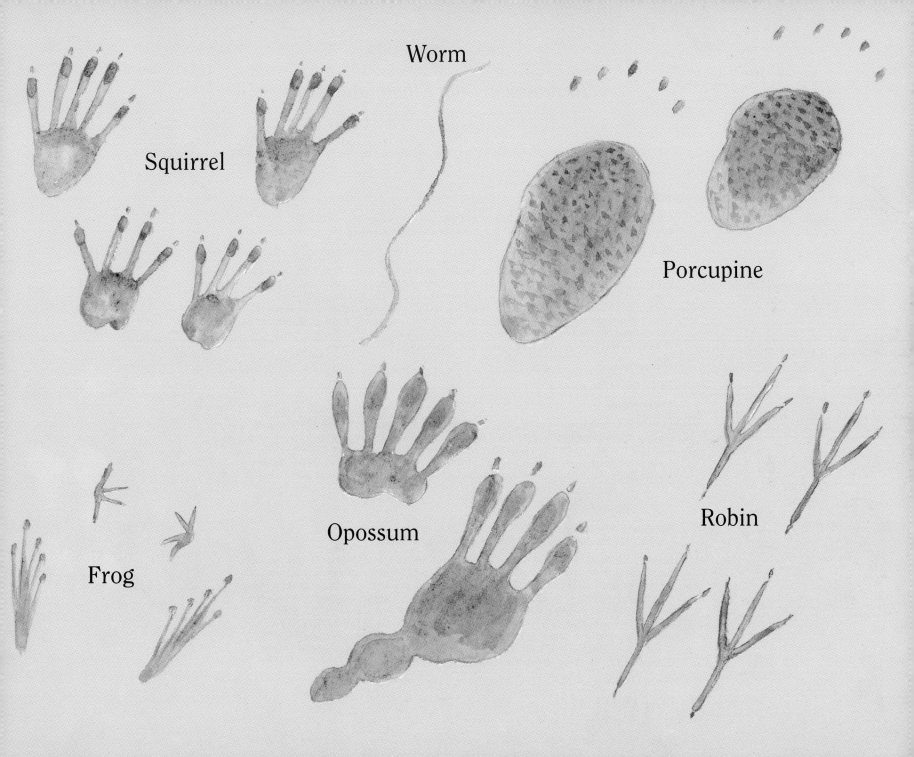

Squirrel

Worm

Porcupine

Frog

Opossum

Robin

To Amanda, Lily, Ethan, and Alex

Acknowledgments

For each of the selections listed below, grateful acknowledgment is made for permission to excerpt and/or reprint original or copyrighted material, as follows:

Text

1 *Animal Tracks,* written and illustrated by Arthur Dorros. Copyright © 1991 by Arthur Dorros. Reprinted by permission of Scholastic, Inc. **32** "Fast Facts: Cottontails," from August 1994 *Ranger Rick* magazine. Copyright © 1994 by the National Wildlife Federation. Reprinted by permission. **36** "Whatsit?," by Anker Odum, from November 1993 *Owl* magazine. Copyright © 1993 by Owl Communications, Toronto. Reprinted by permission. **38** "Hiding," from January 1994 *Your Big Backyard* magazine. Copyright © 1984 by the National Wildlife Federation. Reprinted by permission.

Illustrations

36–37 Anker Odum.

Photography

i Lewis/West Stock. **ii** Courtesy of Arthur Dorros (r, bl); Tracey Wheeler (background). **32** Rod Planck; Frans Lanting/Minden Pictures (cover). **33** Rod Planck (l); Rich Kirchner (r). **34** Leonard Lee Rue III (tl, tc, tr); Paul Rezendes (bl). **35** Rod Planck (l); Gay Bumgarner/Tony Stone Images (r). **36** Val Corbett/Tony Stone Images (cover). **38** Jeff Foott (cover); James H. Carmichael (tr); Dwight Kuhn (bl); Karl H. Switem (br).

1997 Impression

Houghton Mifflin Edition, 1996
Copyright © 1996 by Houghton Mifflin Company. All rights reserved.

Printed in the U.S.A.

ISBN 0-395-73167-4

9-B-98 97

Animal Tracks

Written and illustrated by
Arthur Dorros

HOUGHTON MIFFLIN COMPANY

BOSTON

ATLANTA   DALLAS   GENEVA, ILLINOIS   PALO ALTO   PRINCETON

When you go into the forest, the animals may be hiding. But you can tell which animals are in the forest by looking at their tracks.

Who made tracks in the soft mud by the stream?

A raccoon was looking for food.
Look out, crayfish, or you will be the raccoon's breakfast!

Who made tracks from the reeds to the water?

A family of ducks waddled from their nest in the reeds.

But who made tracks even smaller than
the ducklings' feet?

A frog made the tracks as it hopped along
with small front feet and bigger hind feet.

A turtle is warming up in the sun.
Who made tracks almost as big as the turtle?

A deer walked to the stream to drink.

Some of the tracks are not easy to see.
Where an animal stepped on hard ground, rocks, or plants
there may be no tracks, or only part of a track.

Who scared the deer and made tracks
up the stream bank?

10

A fox chased a rabbit along the stream bank.

Where the rabbit ran, the tracks are far apart.
The rabbit hopped far with each jump.
The rabbit made it home this time.

The fox looks at her reflection in a puddle.
Whose tracks are curving lines in the mud
around the puddle?

A worm is slithering along.
Watch out, worm. Watch out, cricket!
A bird is hopping, looking for a meal.

Nearby is a tree that looks as if it has been chewed.
Who eats trees for lunch?

14

A porcupine ate tree bark until she was full.
Then she walked slowly away.
Porcupines don't have to move fast.
Who would bother a porcupine?

The black bear won't bother the porcupine.
He is busy eating berries.

Then he will rub and scratch on his favorite tree.
The scratches show that he has been there.
The scratches are called a "sign."

Who left another animal sign — teeth marks
on a fallen tree?

A beaver chewed the tree to cut it down.
Beavers drag branches away to build their
round lodge home and a beaver dam.
Behind the dam is a beaver pond.

Who lives among the tall grasses by the beaver pond?

A heron looks for fish to eat.
Muskrats are eating grass.
They leave a sign — a raft of chewed grass
floating in the water.

SLAP! A beaver's tail hits the water,
warning of danger.
Who is making crackling noises in the bushes
by the pond?

A dog runs along a trail, followed by people. Each person leaves a different-sized track. There are small tracks and larger tracks made by small feet and larger feet.

Near a lake are tracks made in sand by bare feet.
Along the road there are muddy tire tracks.
A car is going toward a city.

Cities can be good places to find animal tracks.

Listen carefully, and look for animal signs.
Snow, soft sand, mud, and dust are good places
to look for tracks.

You might even find tracks of animals
that can live in cities, but usually stay hidden —
raccoons, muskrats, or opossums.
Once people even found mountain lion tracks
in a city park!

Be a track detective.
Guess who made *these* tracks in a city park?

29

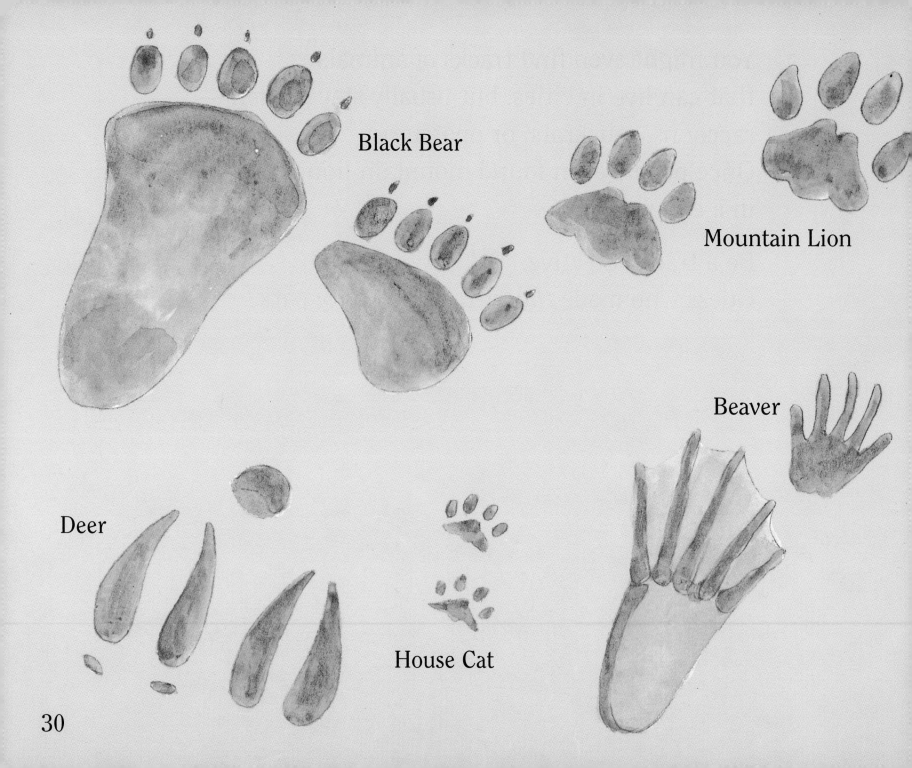

Black Bear

Mountain Lion

Beaver

Deer

House Cat

Great Blue Heron

Dog

Duck

Rabbit

Human Being

Fast Facts
Cottontails
by Claire Miller

Excellent Ears

A cottontail can turn its ears to catch the smallest sounds. This is especially useful for picking up the noises of sneaking enemies.

Ranger Rick

Desert Cottontail